Old Toffer's
BOOK OF
Consequential
DOGS

FABER AND FABER has published children's books since 1929. Some of our very first publications included *Old Possum's Book of Practical Cats* by T. S. Eliot starring the now world-famous Macavity, and *The Iron Man* by Ted Hughes. Our catalogue at the time said that 'it is by reading such books that children learn the difference between the shoddy and the genuine'. We still believe in the power of reading to transform children's lives.

About the Author

Christopher Reid is the author of many books of poems, including *A Scattering* (winner of the Costa Book of the Year Award 2009), *The Song of Lunch*, *Nonsense* and *The Curiosities*. For his first collection of poems for children, *All Sorts*, he received the Signal Award 2000. In 2008 the American Academy of Arts and Letters presented him with the Michael Braude Award for Light Verse. From 1991 to 1999 he was poetry editor at Faber and Faber, where T. S. Eliot once worked.

About the Illustrator

Elliot Elam lives in London. Over the years he has illustrated for the BBC, Channel 4 Television, *The Big Issue*, *The Guardian*, Penguin Books, Victoria University Press and more. Elliot has also painted theatre sets, and built carnival floats at Disneyland. He illustrated the cover for *Six Bad Poets*, also by Christopher Reid.

First published in 2018
by Faber & Faber Limited
Bloomsbury House
74–77 Great Russell Street
London, WC1B 3DA

Typeset by Faber
Printed and bound in China by C&C Offset Printing Co. Ltd
All rights reserved
Text © Christopher Reid, 2018
Illustrations © Elliot Elam, 2018
Patterned endpapers © Shutterstock

The right of Christopher Reid and Elliot Elam to be
identified as author and illustrator of this work respectively
has been asserted in accordance with Section 77 of the
Copyright, Designs and Patents Act 1988

A CIP record for this book is available
from the British Library

ISBN 978–0–571–33409–4

2 4 6 8 10 9 7 5 3 1

Old Toffer's
BOOK OF
Consequential
DOGS

Christopher Reid

Drawings by Elliot Elam

ff

FABER & FABER

Contents

A Rowdy Assembly

First, an explanatory word.

Quite possibly you will have heard

Of Mr T. S. Eliot,

A gentleman who wrote a lot

Of poems about London Cats,

Their habits and their habitats,

Their fanciful and florid names,

Their exploits, dark deeds, pranks and games.

He put these poems in his *Book*

Of Practical Cats. Go, take a look:

You're bound to learn a thing or two.

It's stuffed with facts, some of them true –

Or partly true – or not *all* lies;

Cat secrets likely to surprise

The most informed Ailurophile;

And cat jokes that will bring a smile

To even the stern Ailurophobe

(A character as glum as Job).

Ailurophobe? Ailurophile?

I'm trying to imitate the style

Of T.S.E., who thought it fun

To faze and flummox everyone

With far-fetched and old-fangled words,

Nowadays strictly for the birds;

But, knowing the dictionary by heart,

He versified them with an art

That I can't match; so let's get back,

Quick as we can, on the right track …

Practical Cats is wise and witty,

And all agree it was a pity

He never wrote the book he'd mooted

Of *Consequential Dogs*, which suited

His genius, surely, just as well,

Dogs being, you might say, parallel –

Or mirrorwise – or contrary

To cats. As all the world can see,

Dog is the opposite of cat,

As thin is the opposite of fat,

Or round the opposite of flat,

Or shoe the opposite of hat,

Or ball the opposite of bat,

Or this the opposite of that.

So, to achieve a fairer view,

Not cat or dog alone will do

But both must be placed side by side,

Contrasting points identified,

And their whole wealth of gifts and talents

Totted up and shown to balance.

With this in mind, albeit humbly,

I've rounded up a rowdy assembly

Of my own Consequential Dogs

As counterparts to Eliot's mogs.

Mine are a rough and ready bunch:

You wouldn't take them out to lunch

At some snoot-uppity restaurant,

Or introduce them to an Aunt

You hope might leave you heaps of money;

But if they strike you as friendly, funny,

Full of bounce and fond of a romp,

Forgetful of poetic pomp,

I trust you'll take them as you find them

And, at the very least, not mind them.

The Naming of Dogs

The Naming of Dogs is no difficult matter:

   They're not choosy like cats, they aren't fussy at all.

Simply give them a name, as you'd hand them a platter

   Of scraps from the table or toss them a ball.

Whatever you call them, they're perfectly happy;

   Quite honestly, it would be hard to go wrong,

For they're equally pleased with a name short and snappy

   Or sesquipedalian (long word for long).

Geoff, Wilf and Biff I have always thought suitable

   For stout, stubby terriers, Jack Russells and such,

And the virtue of Brutus is scarcely disputable

   In the case of Rottweilers (do *you* care for them much?).

Horatio and Humphrey for dogs with authority,

   Scrapper and Scruff for your mutts and your tykes,

Benjy, Fred, Buster, Anubis, O'Flaherty

  And Rude Boy are dog names that every dog likes.

So much for the males. Now let's turn to the bitches,

  For whom there are hundreds – no, *thousands* of choices:

Such a storehouse of nomenclaturial riches

  That to chant them all now would exhaust our poor voices.

Just one thing to remember: a name that sounds feline –

  Like Slinkamalina or Tabbytumtat –

Will have any she-puppy making a beeline

  For the nearest escape route, so *don't* give her that!

When you first get your dog and are thinking of naming it,

  There are not many traps that you need to avoid,

But while there is never a danger of shaming *it*,

  You could shame yourself – and feel mighty annoyed

By the looks you receive, of amazement or merriment,

  As you shout in the park at your frolicking hound:

'Cuddles!' or 'Smoochums!' That sort of experiment

Should only be tried when there's no one around.

Dogs themselves, though, are easy to satisfy, seeing

That any old name can be called a success

If ears twitch in response – the one sadness being

They won't answer with yours (and they couldn't care less).

Flo: The Philosophical Foxhound

Foxhounds are better known for sport

Than for profundity of thought;

    Flo is different,

Being of a strong intellectual bent

    And self-taught.

How she got to be this way

Her folks are at a loss to say:

Her mother, Dot, and father, Tinker,

Struggle for words to explain how they

    Brought up a thinker.

'We kept her well away from books,'

   Tinker insists. 'Right, Dot?

No foxhunter wants a swot

In their pack. Now look what we've got –

An intellectual prodigy!

   It has to be

One of them genetic flukes . . .'

True, rather than chasing after foxes,

Brain-bamboozlers and paradoxes

   Occupy Flo's mind:

Why do cats love jumping into boxes? –

   Puzzles of that kind.

And what is the *stickness* of a stick?

Throw her one, she'll run double-quick,

   Not to retrieve it,

Just to stare

At it lying there

As if she can scarcely believe it.

But don't imagine she's dim or thick!

Her powerful mind works all the time

On problems mundane and sublime

That others ignore,

Like: What are shoes for

If not to chew?

And: Why are dog biscuits always too few?

And: Is trashing flowerbeds fun or a crime?

In fact, she works so very hard

On her theories

She's philosophically avant-garde:

Ahead of all the brainiest Professors

Who, by comparison, are idle guessers

And off with the fairies.

For years we've lived in expectation

Of Flo's first, major publication,

Presenting her reports

On everything a dog should know

And titled, possibly, *The Flow of Thoughts*;

Or, *The Thoughts of Flo*.

She may be slow

But the book will be a revelation!

Heath, Hill, Park and Street

The Dogs on the Heath

Say the Dogs on the Hill

Have the sharpest of teeth

And will fight to the kill;

While the Dogs on the Hill

Say the Dogs in the Park

Bear the whole world ill will,

You can tell by their bark;

And the Dogs in the Park

Say the Dogs in the Street

Go berserk after dark

And are fast on their feet;

And the Dogs in the Street

CHRISTOPHER REID

Say the Dogs on the Heath

Are the worst you could meet

With *their* terrible teeth;

But when a Dog of the Heath

Sees a Dog of the Hill –

Or the Park – or the Street –

It's a joy, it's a thrill,

It's a scrumbunctious treat,

And each rushes to greet

His new friend with a bark;

And they can't get their fill

Of this play-fighting lark,

This scrimmage and spill,

First one underneath,

Then the other, until

Owners call, and they beat

A reluctant retreat,

HEATH, HILL, PARK AND STREET

Tails wagging still;

And the Dog of the Heath

Goes back to the Heath,

And you hear him repeat

That the Dogs on the Hill

Have the sharpest of teeth

And will fight to the kill;

While the Dogs on the Hill . . .

Lola's Circus

As quite a young pup, Lola already knew

What she wanted – and very much didn't – to do:

What she very much didn't was to live in a flat

With a couple, their children, TV and a cat;

What she even more did was to break out and see

The whole Wide, Wild World – where a dog could
     be free!

Walks in the park on the end of a lead

Fell a long way short of fulfilling this need,

As did countryside drives in the back of a car –

From which a small puppy can seldom see far:

You might as well sit counting drops of rain

As they dribble and drool down a windowpane!

LOLA'S CIRCUS

Which was how she'd spent many an afternoon . . .

But then life unexpectedly changed its tune

With the wonderful news buzzing up and down

That the world's greatest circus had come to town –

Rumbustikoff's Fabulous Animal Circus –

And, what was more, they were looking for workers.

That very same evening, Lola leapt

From a first-floor balcony, landed, and kept

Running until she reached Finsbury Park

Where the circus tent stood. It was now after dark,

But the lights were bright and the music was loud,

Attracting a large, excitable crowd.

'What now?' Lola thought; then, not far off,

Saw the Maestro himself, Rumbustikoff.

'Can you give me a job?' she asked him, boldly.

LOLA'S CIRCUS

At first, he peered at her rather coldly:

'We don't exactly,' he said, 'have oodles

Of opportunities for French Poodles.'

Then a smile altered the set of his face:

'I can, however, offer a place

As Knife-thrower's Assistant. Could you do that?

Our last Assistant, a Siamese Cat,

Disappeared this morning, I've no idea why.'

'I'll be happy,' said Lola, 'to give it a try!'

Now, the job of a Knife-thrower's Assistant is this:

To stand still while all his thrown knives *just* miss,

Thunking left, thunking right, not quite grazing her body –

And woe betide her if his throwing is shoddy!

Brave Lola stood still as a statue, as ordered,

And the audience, awed by her *hauteur*, applauded.

So she now had a job and was cock-a-hoop

To be joining Rumbustikoff's Circus. The troupe

Broke camp next day and continued its tour,

Town by town. Lola's earnings were poor –

A Knife-thrower's Assistant is never well paid –

But her new life was one long circus parade!

Lola's Circus

And the whole Wide, Wild World was hers at last!

Being good at her job, too, Lola rose fast

Through the circus ranks. Very soon, she learnt

To jump through flaming hoops without getting burnt

And to skip along a tightrope without falling off –

Hugely impressing Rumbustikoff.

One morning, as she was taming a lion,

The Maestro told her: 'I've had my eye on

You for some time: your clowning's great fun;

Last night, when I saw you shot from the gun,

I said to myself, "That girl will go far!";

And your trapeze work marks you out as a star.

'There seems to be nothing that you can't do:

Please allow me to give my Circus to you.

I'm getting old and my one requirement

LOLA'S CIRCUS

Is to name my successor before retirement;

Let me leave the whole lot in your capable paws:

Only say yes – and it will be yours!'

'Yes!' said Lola, without hesitation;

Since when, she has toured not just the nation

But every part of the Wide, Wild World

With brass band barrumphing and banners unfurled,

Rightly proud of her Circus's global renown.

Don't fail to catch it when it's next in town!

Dobson: The Dog Detective

Universally acknowledged as a Hero of our Time,

Dobson, the Dog Detective, sworn enemy of crime,

Uses his own odd methods to nab and bring to book

Villains of every type, from mastermind to petty crook.

Police Dogs play a vital role in criminal detection

With their superior powers of olfactory inspection –

Not to mention four-legged running (a trick we sadly lack),

And employing jaws and teeth to drag escaping wrong 'uns back.

Dobson, by striking contrast, spends all day in his bed,

Slumped there so motionlessly you might well think him dead,

Till a snuffle or a wheeze disturbs his very ample frame

And you know the clever fellow has in mind a different game.

There was a time when Dobson, as a young and eager Beagle,

Dashed out with the other dogs in hot pursuit of the illegal

And thereby helped to catch his share of bent and shady types,

Doggedly (*yes!*) and dutifully earning his Sergeant's stripes.

When, after further service, he rose to be Inspector,

His behaviour underwent a change that could easily have

      wrecked (or

At least called into question) a lesser dog's career:

'I'm off to bed,' he told them. 'And I'll be staying there!'

Though he has rarely left it since, there was never cause

      for worry.

He does things in his own sweet time, you cannot make

      him hurry;

Days, weeks and months pass in a doze, then suddenly he'll cry:

'I know not just who did the deed, but how, and when, and why!'

His mighty and mysterious brain has been active all along,

And, what is quite extraordinary, he never gets things wrong:

The most ingenious criminals (cats, to a large degree)

Thanks to Dobson and his dozing are now under lock and key.

Dobson: The Dog Detective

So, when a crime's uncovered and the Force is in a rush

To identify the culprit, please don't disturb his hush.

If you see his blanket slipping, gently put it back in place

And step away on tip-toe – because Dobson's on the case!

Boffo Dogs

One day, one of them will surprise you,

So it's my duty to advise you

    Of their existence.

Boffo Dogs are none too bright,

It's often hard to see the light

In their small brains, and you would be right

    To keep your distance.

Boffo Dogs are full of joy,

But Boffo Dogs are apt to annoy

    Through their excess

Of eagerness to show affection,

To give your person nosy inspection,

And hurl themselves in every direction

    Making a mess.

BOFFO DOGS

Boffo Dogs, being fit and feisty,

Know neither discipline nor nicety

   Of etiquette:

Open the door, they're through it first

With an unnecessary burst

Of barking; their manners are the worst

   Of any pet.

Boffo Dogs are brash and bold,

Boffos cannot be controlled:

   One of their tricks –

Respecting neither time nor place –

Is, soon as spot you, up they'll race

To claw your chest and flannel your face

   With big damp licks.

Boffo Dogs

Boffo Dogs are horribly hearty,

Boffo Dogs are ready to party

    All night long:

Swinging tails and stamping the floor,

Never mind the folks next door

Who want to sleep, at half past four

    They're still going strong.

Boffo Dogs are mad for fun,

Boffo Dogs treat everyone

    As their best friend.

Beware! Possessing vast amounts

Of *joie de vivre*, brim-full of bounce,

There's always a Boffo ready to pounce

    Round the next bend.

Howling Jenny

The great Dog Singers of a bygone age

     Can still be heard on CD or downloaded:

Stars of the jazz club or the opera stage,

Growlers and belters who were once the rage,

     Sing on in styles exotic and outmoded.

Figures almost of legend or of myth,

     Like Rags, the only Scottie known to rival

The swing of Lady Day or Bessie Smith,

Or Sam the Pug, who earned comparison with

     Caruso, certainly deserve survival.

Others, however, are forgotten now,

    And it's a bitterness to think how many:

Big Raoul, for instance, whose baritone bow-wow

We'll never get to hear, because somehow

    No one recorded it – and Howling Jenny.

Yet I recall a moment in my youth

    (Oh yes, I had one) when I may have heard

Jenny herself, grizzled and long in the tooth,

And, while it's hard to disentangle truth

    From wishfulness, I'll tell you what occurred.

It must have been the middle of the day.

    I'd wandered into some suburban pub

To get a spot of lunch (or anyway

A drink). Very few customers, and they

    Were silent, busy with their booze and grub.

HOWLING JENNY

A man walked in, pulling a Labrador

    On a rope leash. He went straight to the bar,

Ordered two pints, put one down on the floor

(For the dog), drank his, ordered one more

    And drank that. Nothing unusual, so far . . .

What happened next is what has stayed with me.

    In those days, every public-house saloon

Boasted an upright piano, an elderly,

Coffinlike jangle-box that you were free

    To play, if you didn't mind it out of tune.

The man sat down at it, dog at his side.

    He vamped a chord or two, whereupon the hound

Threw back her head, shut both eyes, opened wide

Her mouth – and a wail that might have been *Abide*

    With Me emerged: the most unearthly sound!

Howling Jenny

Could Jenny in great age have made that row?

    A far, faint note of sweetness in her song,

The doddery grace with which she took her bow,

Convinced me then, but there is no one now

    Who can confirm it, and I may be wrong.

Leopold: Prince of Lap Dogs

Leopold is a languid chap,

Lazing all day on a lady's lap,

Lounging and lolling all day long,

While under his breath he sings this song:

'Look at me, look at me, everyone!

I am the luckiest dog in the world,

Lying here, out of the heat of the sun,

Lying here, having the greatest fun –

Nothing but lying indoors all day,

No need to go outdoors to play!

Carefree, cosseted and curled

All day long on a comfy lap,

Oh, am I not the luckiest chap?'

Leopold is a Pekingese,

And all day long he takes his ease;

The principal perk of a Pekingese is

Doing precisely as he pleases,

And if it happens that Leo chooses

To snore his day away in snoozes,

No one can tell him that he's wrong –

As you'll learn from verse two of his song:

'I am the great Prince Leopold,

And I live in the lap of luxury,

Where I do as I want, and *won't* be told!

If I have a mind to take a nap

At ten in the morning, or half past three

In the afternoon, on this lovely lap,

That is precisely what I shall do,

Just as you would – wouldn't you? –

If you were a Lap Dog Prince like me.'

LEOPOLD: PRINCE OF LAP DOGS

Leo's whole life is lazy and lax:

Only breaks for meals and snacks

Interrupt his daylong dozes;

But when at last night comes and closes

The eyes of dogs who *do* get out

Into broad daylight – gadding about

And making friends with other dogs,

Joining in yappy dialogues,

Sniffing and scampering and scrapping,

Then Leopold, no longer napping,

Lies alone in his little bed,

And a last, sad verse runs through his head:

'I am poor, lonely Leopold:

Look at me, look at me, and behold

A creature cruelly misused,

Far from the lap where I once snoozed

And lapped up every cuddle and kiss!

Cast out from love and into the cold,

Under five cashmere blankets, I

Bewail the betrayal of my bliss,

Languish in anguish, and sob and sigh!'

Towzle versus the Trainers

Towzle's a sort of a Cockapoo.

    A Cockawhat? A Whatapoo?

Do I really have to explain it to you?

    Yes, please do!

Well, it means that he's a Designer Dog.

    Designer Dog?

    Will you kindly stop

Interrupting this barely started monologue?

Yes, Designer Dog: that's a fancy way

Of saying mongrel, a mix, a muddle

Of Cocker Spaniel and Miniature Poodle,

    Though, in Towzle's case,

I suspect there's an extra something too,

And his great-grandfather may have been

A Bale of Hay,

And his great-grandmother a Kitchen Mop.

Look at his face:

It can't be seen,

For all the fur and moustache and eyebrows there,

Though occasionally a tongue pokes out

Making it clear

That that's his snout

And not the tail end.

Now, Towzle's everybody's friend –

Unless you happen to be a shoe.

A shoe?

Didn't I just say to you . . .?

Sorry. Do continue.

Yes, a shoe, or slipper, or boot,

Or anything else a person might put

On his or her foot,

Towzle versus the Trainers

Footwear generally

Being his enemy,

Maddening him and making him snarl and snap

In a manner that's puzzling

From such a sweet-natured and soft-hearted chap.

Time and again, I've observed him nuzzling

And sniffing an empty plimsoll, or abandoned pump,

When all of a sudden back he'll jump

And start to yap

Shrilly and heroically, as if to say:

'Come on! Come and get me – *if you dare!*'

Thus the shoe,

Petrified with fear,

Is kept at bay.

But . . .

Kindly keep your mouth shut

While I tell you what happened the other night,

When a pair of Trainers made the mistake

    Of crossing Towzle's path.

    Nobody was awake

    To see the actual fight,

    Just the aftermath:

    A gruesome sight –

Two newish Trainers, each almost as big as our lad,

    Mercilessly chewed,

    Mauled and mangled,

    Efficiently strangled

    With their own laces,

Flung aside and left to die

    In different places . . .

    When interviewed,

    Towzle couldn't see

    That he'd done anything bad,

Only what a Cockapoo

Is predisposed to do

When there's nobody to restrain him.

Could it be . . .

What is it now? Speak up!

Could it be

Your murderous pup

Went mad

Because those Trainers tried to train him?

Well, possibly . . .

Molly: A Dog of the Night

Most dogs are Larks, but a few are Owls – by which I mean
to say,

That, for every nine hundred and ninety-nine who favour
the light of day,

There's always one who will wait till it's dark before
running out to play.

Though a Dog of the Night is a rare enough beast,

I'm the trusted friend of one, at least,

And the tales she tells of her nocturnal strolls

Through parts of town overrun by Trolls

And other Monsters you'd not care to meet

Grouching towards you down some dark street

Are apt to make my hair stand on end

Out of fear for the safety of my dear friend.

But Molly herself is quite without fear, and will not

      renounce the habit:

As a Lurcher who since puppyhood has done for many a

      rabbit,

Her first reponse to any threat is to give chase and to nab it.

   So, when all the rest of the family

   Are snug in bed, as they should be,

   And Molly, no longer pretending to nap,

   Has scampered to find the secret gap

   Through which she can wriggle out for her walk

   (Yes, I know where it is but I've sworn not to talk,

   And – let me repeat – I'm a *trusted* friend),

   Any Troll that comes grumphing round the bend

   Will know that she's famous for speed and bite,

   And the worst he will do is to snarl a polite,

   'Hello, Molly. Have a nice night.'

By now you're probably dying to ask, how does Molly fare

With the Ghosts and Ghouls and other Ghastlies that

whoop through London's night air?

The simple fact of the matter is that nothing gives her a scare.

If a Headless Duke comes flitting by,

She'll look him steadily in the eye

(The one peering out from the crook of his arm),

For how could she possibly come to harm

From something as flimsy as a Ghost?

A slight embarrassment, at most,

To catch him carrying his own head

When a page should be doing that instead . . .

Vampires, as they hurtle past

Silently and very fast,

On their way to nipping people's necks,

Slow down to pay her their respects;

Likewise, their cousins, the Acro Bats;

While Cat Burglars and burgling Cats

Pause their nefarious pursuits,

And (actual) Owls send out sweet hoots,

As she proceeds on her patrol:

The whole night world has welcomed Moll!

Even the Moon and Stars above

Peep through the murk, to show their love.

Frazzlesprat

Consider the plight of Frazzlesprat,

A dog who wanted to be a cat –

Or thought he was one anyhow

And went about shouting 'Miao-wow-wow!'

(Or occasionally 'Bow-wow-miao!')

At any person in the vicinity

Inclined to question his felinity.

Frazzlesprat wasn't his given name;

That was Spot, but who can blame

The lad for changing it: Spot is *not*

A proper cat name. 'Would Eliot

Have dreamt of putting a cat called Spot

Into a poem?' he used to say,

When arguing his case: 'No way!'

Fair enough, but changing a name

And changing one's nature are not the same,

And Frazzlesprat had work to do

Convincing obstinate doubters, who,

It must be said, were quite a few,

So counterintuitive was his theory, all

Dogs are potential cat material.

Which was even less likely in relation

To a large and gangly-limbed Dalmatian

Such as Frazzlesprat was (or used to be):

Sitting on a fence, climbing a tree,

Tricks that come automatically

To cats *born* as cats, are hard to pick up

For even the most adventuresome pup.

FRAZZLESPRAT

Let doubters doubt, though, and scoffers scoff,

Frazzlesprat wouldn't be put off!

Wearing lots of spots but not much fur,

Prone to growl when he wanted to purr –

Shortcomings like that could never deter

Our hero from his improbable calling;

And he *did* get the hang of caterwauling.

If you want a moral from my tale,

Try this for size: it's fine to fail,

Especially if you do it with style:

Frazzlesprat may have been in denial,

But he made an entire family smile

With his catlike attitudes around the house.

(And once he almost caught a mouse.)

Jack and Jill: A Pair of Mutts

Tell me, what are they truly worth,

Those dogs of so-called noble birth:

Offspring of an unbroken line

Whose forefathers sat down to dine

With William of Normandy,

Since when they have held themselves to be

Superior to the whole pack

Of common-or-garden Jill and Jack?

Or those who grew from pampered pups

To carry off rosettes and cups

At international competitions

Through the dark artistry of beauticians,

JACK AND JILL: A PAIR OF MUTTS

Shampooers and manicurists:

Praised by connoisseurs and purists,

Are they even a haircut above

The scruffy mutts you and I love?

Let me sing the exploits of Jack,

Who, thrown a ball, will bring it back

Five hundred times an afternoon;

He loves to bark at any moon;

And isn't it a splendid thing

To snap a bluebottle on the wing

And swallow it whole? (You don't agree?

Try it yourself and *then* you'll see . . .)

Jill's accomplishments are no fewer:

She is a champion chair-leg chewer,

Likes nothing more than a roll in muck,

Takes to water like a duck –

A duck that sends up drenching splashes –

And, when the doorbell ding-dongs, dashes

Straight to chase the intruder off

With woofs as harsh as whooping cough.

Next to these, the aristocrats

Of pedigree might as well be *cats*,

They're so unlike the real thing;

Same goes for glamour-puss dogs who bring

Trophies home to vaunt their glory:

They are irrelevant to the story

Of madcap Jack and messy Jill,

Two dogs of whom I'll hear no ill.

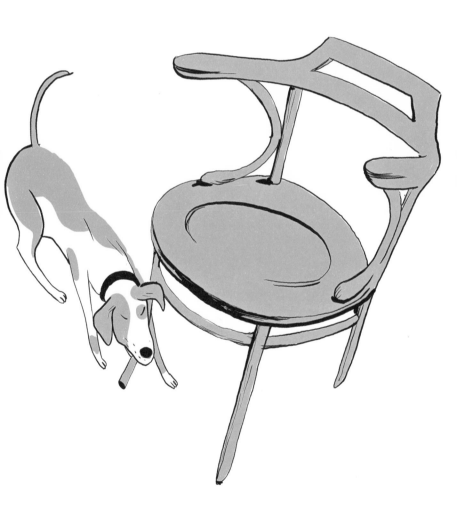

Praise Song
for Ballybeg Rosie

O great Greyhound,

You're no Stayhound

Or Delayhound:

Up flies the starting-gate

And you're an Offandawayhound!

Speed is your knack,

You race

And outpace

All other runners,

While off the track

You outgrace

All other stunners.

If we look at you

Praise Song for Ballybeg Rosie

Face to face

You're barely there:

So narrow to see,

As un-3D

As a dog can realistically be;

But your profile,

From tail's cursive curve

To long, tooth-baring

And tongue-cooling smile,

Is pure style:

Bone, muscle, nerve

On full display,

Least possible waist,

No flesh to spare –

More sketch in air

Than statue,

Lean, lithe

Praise Song for Ballybeg Rosie

Silhouette

Sharper than a scythe

And made for a single purpose:

Haste.

Beautiful in repose,

You're more so at speed.

Do you really intend,

Or need,

To catch and fetch

That silly electric hare,

That thing of fluff?

You bet!

Dashing, daring

Darling of the crowd

That roars so loud

As you take the bend

And streak for the finishing-post,

You thrill us with your one-track mind

And super strength,

All at the service

Of leaving the pack behind

And being foremost:

A win by a nose

Never good enough –

It must be at least a length!

Benbow's Ghost

Not many can boast that they've seen Benbow's Ghost,

    Fewer still that they've heard him speak,

But I'm one of those few, so let me tell you

    Exactly what happened last week.

I was down by the River and starting to shiver,

    The night being cold and damp,

When a most eerie sound made me halt, spin around,

    And search the road with my lamp:

A road without feature, with no living creature,

    Just high brick walls on each side

And, between them, unending drizzle descending . . .

    I was totally mystified!

Turning back to resume my trudge through the gloom,

    I heard the sound once more:

Benbow's Ghost

Part howl and part moan, part yelp and part groan,

    It made me spin round, as before.

There, a few feet away and seeming to sway

    As if tipsy and caught by surprise,

Stood a vast, shaggy dog, formed entirely from fog

    And with embers in place of eyes!

My first thought was to run (wouldn't anyone

    In a similar awkward position?),

Except I could feel a strong, unvoiced appeal

    From this canine apparition.

Then (and this is no joke) he actually spoke

    In a voice that was friendly, if gruff:

'Belay there!' he said. 'I may be long dead,

    But my thirst remains lively enough.

What would you think if I suggested a drink?

    There's an old seamen's inn, The Ship,

That keeps special hours, and this damnable shower's

    Beginning to give me the pip.'

I agreed, and quite soon we were in the saloon

    Of The Ship with tankards of ale

And a crackling log fire to help us get drier,

    While the ghostly dog told me his tale:

Benbow's Ghost

'Benbow's the name. I achieved some small fame

    From my exploits at sea years ago.

I've no wish to tattle, but there's many a battle

    They'd have lost without me, you know:

Gnashing and gnawing away in the thick of the fray,

    I always led the fighting;

Hundreds of foreign legs owe their wooden pegs

    To my superior biting.

When Drake interfered with the King of Spain's beard,

    It was me that supplied the matches –

So the Spanish fleet, they'd beat a retreat,

    Battening down all hatches,

If ever they knew I was one of the crew

    Aboard some man-o'-war;

And later, the Dutch, who don't scare at much,

    Would jump and swim for the shore

If they fell afoul of my menacing growl

CHRISTOPHER REID

Bearing down on them over the ocean;

The French as well, though like Fiends out of Hell,

Would set up a right commotion,

Wheeling about in a panicky rout

To escape my merciless jaws.

That's how – don't you see? – throughout history,

I battled with scarcely a pause;

But then somehow I struck a run of ill luck,

Being slow to understand

That the foolish Sea Dog who's too fond of his grog

Is doomed to fetch up on dry land.'

There he stopped, and I saw his phantom forepaw

Mime the act of raising a glass,

While his nebulous face pulled a rueful grimace;

I nodded; he continued: 'Alas,

That Sea Dog was me and, without the sea,

I was at my addled wits' end.

Benbow's Ghost

It may be the case that dry land is the place

    For lubbers like you, my friend,

But the rolling wave is the one thing I crave,

    And without it I was on the shelf:

Left to degrade and obscurely fade

    To the ghost of my former self,

Which is what you see here ...'

                  His eyes went blear,

    His voice faltered, his dim old shape

Disappeared wholly, and, not too slowly,

    I effected my own escape.

Doggerel and Wagtail

When Doggerel came to London

    As a young, ambitious pup,

His head was full of poems,

    He couldn't stop making them up.

This was the Sixteenth Century,

    When every dog wrote verse,

And many were forced to scribble

    To fill an empty purse.

Puppies know almost nothing,

    But puppies have no fear:

So long as their noses command them,

    They follow anywhere.

Doggerel's nose was exceptional,

   London was full of stinks,

And it's not uncommon for a puppy

   To write faster than he thinks.

Poems on every kind of smell

   And of every size and shape

Flowed from his hyperactive quill

   And made all London gape.

Soon he was rich and famous,

   Toast of the Taverns and the Court,

Till some older (and envious) dogs stepped in

   To spoil his sport.

'Has anybody thought to ask,' they asked,

   'If his poems are any good?

DOGGEREL AND WAGTAIL

Aren't they far too easy to like,

    And too easily understood?

'Where are the learned allusions?

    Where are the Latin and Greek?

What is the value of a piece of verse

    That any cur can speak?'

'Oh, yes,' said the rest of London;

    'We see just what you mean.'

And Doggerel's fame faded there and then

    As if it had never been.

Only a certain Wagtail,

    Another young pup of the day

With literary ambitions,

    Observed, then scampered away.

And the verse that William Wagtail

    Subsequently wrote

Is full of the Doggerel spirit

    And many a Doggerel quote.

A Wagtail Sonnet

Full long thou bark'st at me, my love, and loud;

Hearing the sound, I do not miss the sense,

That I that once was lovingly bow-wow'd

Must now, unlov'd, bow out and hie me hence;

Loving the bark with which thou didst me woo,

I bark'd back lustily in loving wise,

Unwise though 't was to lend my love to you,

Who, now that love is loth, misprize the prize;

What is a bark but noise, a noisome sound,

Annoying and a nuisance to the ear,

Nagging the hearer, be he man or hound,

Who, hounded and unmann'd, cannot but hear?

    Words are more sweet, and here I proffer proofs,

    One witty word is worth a thousand woofs.

Dog Juan

The dogs of Islington and Camden Town –
   Including Handsome Johnny, Jack the Lad
And others who had earned some small renown
   For amorous exploits (nothing truly bad) –
Were in a flap about this new dog down
   From somewhere in the sticks: what drove them mad
Was that the local girls were one and all
Besotted with him, hopelessly in thrall.

The evidence for this was unignorable:
   When Romeo, a Schnauzer from York Way,
Approached his old flame Juliet, an adorable
   Red Setter from the Cally Road, she'd say,
'Leave me alone!' (or something more deplorable).

'I loved you once, but that was yesterday;

This morning I met Juan; he must be Spanish;

I love him now, so will you kindly vanish?'

Behold the zeal and dash with which, across

    Both northern boroughs, Juan pursued his wooing!

Look at the map, and you would be at a loss

    To account for such athletic froing and toing.

They say a rolling stone gathers no moss,

    But a roaming dog, who knows what he is doing,

Can gather what he wants – though Juan's fast feet

And knack for sweet talk would be hard to beat.

Jealous, the other dogs could not work out

    What made him such a hit with all the bitches.

'Can't be his looks,' they said. 'He's short, he's stout;

    His coat's a mess that he scratches when it itches;

Lopsided ears, an undistinguished snout –

    Nothing is right, yet somehow he bewitches

The female heart. Whatever this boy's got

We want for our own use, and we want a lot!'

As it turned out, they need not have been been worried.

    Dog Juan himself had never meant to stay

And, after several busy weeks, he hurried

    Either to Hackney or to Haringey,

Where there were more hearts waiting to be flurried.

    Our dogs went back to their old, lazy way

Of making love, and their mates were contented,

As if no Juan had ever been seen or scented.

Bess: The Champion Peopledog

Peopledog of the Year

Five years in a row

And uncontested star of the show,

Bess is beyond compare.

I saw her at last year's trials

Which, naturally, she won by miles,

Breaking the record again:

Seventy-seven women,

Eighty-five men

And a hundred and thirteen children

Herded into the pen –

A staggering feat!

You should have heard

BESS: THE CHAMPION PEOPLEDOG

That herd of people bleat,

Asking: 'How did we end up here?

One moment we were innocently

Walking down the street,

Minding our own business,

The next, to our surprise,

We were a mob

Bolting this way and that,

Surrounded by *just one dog*

Not so gently

Chasing and chivvying us,

Sometimes crouching flat

With a bossy look in her eyes,

Sometimes aiming a run

At anyone

Who dared to straggle or stray,

Bewildering us

With her outflankings,

Fancy footwork and feints.

What could we do but obey?

Do you call that *fair*?'

The judges, who were all sheep,

Couldn't have cared less

And frankly ignored

Such complaints,

Dismissing them out of hand

In their eagerness

To honour Bess

With the special award –

Which came with a silver cup

That was hers to keep –

Of Greatest Peopledog in the Land!

Old Bloke

Here, let me introduce you to my old mate Bloke:
He's friendly enough and can take a joke –
Needs to with that name! Course, he didn't choose it,
But he'll grin and bear it when the other lads use it.

Camden born and proud of it – as who wouldn't be?
Funny mix of breeds: take a dekko and see
Bits of this, that and what not, a right old cocktail,
From prize-fighter's flat nose to dinky little docked tail.

Typical family set-up, this London geezer:
Nan was a Mopehound, grandad a Wheezer,
Something else back there, too – Punk Terrier, perhaps? –
But he's no more complicated than the other chaps.

That's the chaps he hangs out with down the pub,

Where they constitute an informal sort of club

For the endless discussion of their team's last game –

Arsenal, stupid! – that, and who to blame.

Time was, Bloke himself used to chase a ball

And dream of selection, but he let that one fall

When his owner stopped throwing it, they both turned to fat,

And there's not much a dog can do about that.

Now a trot to the pub is his only exercise,

Then a wobblier trot home after copious supplies

Of pork scratchings and crisps – Thai Chilli preferred,

Flame Grilled next choice, Cheese and Onion third.

OLD BLOKE

Sustained by this traditional London diet,

Bloke's cheery enough, if inclined to be quiet.

But don't kid yourself there's nothing going on in his brain:

Observe him up close and you'll see it plain.

Most of all, when a pretty pooch saunters by,

There's a straightening of his stance and an ogle in his eye,

Enough to show he's not yet over the hill

And the old dog has old dog in him still.

But then he'll turn back to his mates at the bar

Where they're grumbling on about how the Ref went too far

Awarding that penalty, and he'll nod his big head

Till a tug on his collar has him toddling off to bed.

The Stray

I don't know her name. Do *you* know her name –
   The dog at the end of the street? She's there,
Then she's off at top speed as if playing a game
   Of tag, or chasing after a hare;
But there are no hares in this neighbourhood
   And her nervous bolt looks less like play
Than a wild attempt to vanish for good –
   Which she almost manages, being a Stray.

Rapid exits and vanishing acts
   Are part of any Stray's bag of tricks;
Likewise, a gift for covering tracks
   And escaping from even the tightest fix.
Without a home, without an owner,

THE STRAY

A Stray, to be safe, must keep on her toes

And be true to the faith of outlaw and loner,

   Trusting no one and nothing wherever she goes.

London's a city of lures and traps,

   A labyrinth leading to many dead ends,

And that tasty bone dropped in the alley perhaps

   Was left as a snack by kind-hearted friends,

But equally well could be bait for a Stray

   Made reckless by hunger. Best to leave it alone:

What a terrible shame it would be to fall prey

   To the dog catcher on account of a bone!

Yet she has to eat and she has to sleep.

   Doesn't she sometimes long to be caught?

Apparently not: what makes her keep

   Running has less to do with sport

Than with a strange, erratic compulsion

Which allows her to pick a meagre meal

From a tipped-over bin without revulsion,

   Or under the shade of a brick wall steal

A few minutes' rest, until the whole thing

   Starts up again and she's back on her feet,

Scenting night's threats and ready to spring

   In any direction at all – *toot sweet!*

THE STRAY

So, the dog we glimpsed at the end of the road,

 And couldn't name, has probably not

Chosen to be of no fixed abode;

 It's a mystery, though, what decided her lot

And set her off on this life of flight –

 Forever footloose, destined to roam

As daytime skedaddler and fly-by-night

 Towards an ever-receding home.

Fill Your Home with Happy Hounds!

Fill your home with Happy Hounds!

Better still, fill house and grounds:

Indoors, outdoors, cellar, roof!

A dog-filled home is misery-proof,

So see to it that yours abounds

    In Happy Hounds!

A home with no dog lacks a heart;

A home with one, well, that's a start,

But why stop there when two or three

    Or four

    Or more –

Several on every floor! –

Can join the happy family?

Doglessness is a disgrace,

Absence of dogs a waste of space;

   Dogs are, to be sure,

Not just a source of great felicity

But a prerequisite of domesticity –

Like mains supply, or electricity,

   Or furniture.

I have been into dogless homes;

   They're very strange.

Carpeted voids where no dog roams,

They make you want to rearrange

Everything from top to bottom: an

   Airedale or two

   In the downstairs loo

   To lighten the gloom;

Perhaps a skitter of Whippets to race

Fill Your Home with Happy Hounds!

From room to room;

Or a Wolfhound instead

Of a drab old counterpane on the bed;

Or a Bulldog in place

Of that horrible ottoman . . .

A home without dogs is a poor home,

So don't let it be said of *your* home,

'DOGS NOT ALLOWED'.

Embrace the dog that's friend to man,

Get in as many as you can,

Acquire a crowd!

If you can squeeze in one more Terrier,

Don't hesitate – the more the merrier!

Become the owner of a Noah's Ark

Of dogs alone,

Then, when you've done,

CHRISTOPHER REID

Sit back and let the whole crew bark

    Till the place resounds,

    And you can be proud

To have filled your home with Happy Hounds!

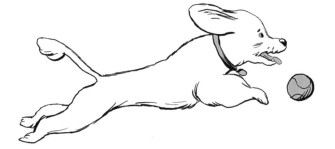